The Little Magritte

Catherine de Duve

in association with the Royal Museums of Fine Arts of Belgium

KATE'ART
EDITIONS

His father Léopold was a merchant and tailor. He sold suits. His mother Regina was a milliner, and until she married she created beautiful hats.

René Magritte was born on 21 November 1898 in Lessines, a little town in Belgium.

René was the oldest of three boys. His little brothers were called Raymond and Paul. When René was very young, his mother died. He never spoke about it. It was far too sad.

Raymond, Paul, René

René Magritte

René's first memory was of a wooden crate that he saw from his crib. Can you see it? René was overwhelmed when one day, a hot-air balloon ended up on the roof of his house.

During a holiday spent at his aunt's, René saw an artist for the first time. He was painting in a cemetery. What a strange place to paint!

René loved to hear the sound of the jingle bells that draft horses wore around their necks. When he was 12, René took drawing lessons just above a sweet shop. What could be more inspiring?

Georgette

When René Magritte was 14 years old, he met Georgette Berger on a merry-go-round at a fair. Nine years later they got married. Georgette was René's *muse*. Here she is, surrounded by everyday objects: a key, a candlestick, a glove, a piece of paper…

A muse is someone who inspires an artist or poet.

Who is this blue woman? A statue? A dream? A Muse? Georgette?

Choose your own muse. Draw her portrait and everyday objects around her.

The Roaring Twenties

'**B**ring on the pianos, saxophones and trombones! Everything is in a whirl, it's the *Roaring Twenties*!'

During the 1920s, jazz started to be played in the night clubs.

Young women bobbed their hair and wore long pearl necklaces that they twirled as they danced to the crazy rhythms of the foxtrot and the charleston.

MAGRITTE

"Minuit"

ne robe du soir créée par Norine

*In the 1920s, known as the '**Roaring Twenties**', women gained more freedom to work outside the home and to dress in more comfortable clothes. They stopped wearing corsets and floor-length dresses, cut their long hair and sometimes even wore trousers! There had never been anything like it! Waltz was abandoned for quick, crazy dances…*

Magritte dreamt of becoming an artist. In 1916, he moved to Brussels and enrolled in the academy of Fine Arts. He tried out different styles of painting… Cubist! Futurist! Abstract!

 Can you see a change in Magritte's style and art technique?

Futurist

Cubist

Abstract

Collage

Impressionist

Gouache

To earn a living, Magritte drew designs for a wallpaper factory. He went on to create advertisements and posters. These were his first paintings that attracted and surprised the viewer.

Look at this poster. What slogan would you add to it?

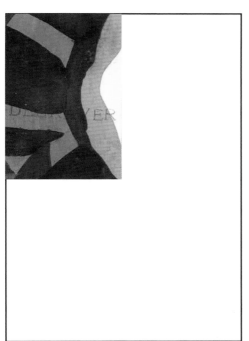

 Finish
the wallpaper
pattern designed
by Magritte.

Wallpaper project

Imagine you are a graphic designer.
Choose your favourite sweet and create
your own advertisement for it.

Surrealist!

De Chirico

In 1925, Magritte saw a work of art by Giorgio De Chirico. 'Now I know what I must paint!' he exclaimed. Surreal scenes! In De Chirico's painting, objects are suspended on a panel in a deserted town. Everything is quiet and mysterious... Soon after, Magritte created his first surrealist works.

Find these details in the picture and make up a story to go with the scene.

In 1927, René and Georgette moved to France, to a town near Paris. Magritte painted a great deal. He met the surrealists Breton, Eluard, Miro, Dali, Arp, Ernst and Man Ray. René and Georgette were invited to stay with Dali in Cadaqués, in Spain. But soon after, Magritte felt that he was on the margins of the French surrealist group and he decided to move back to Belgium.

*The **surrealists** were artists who wanted to change the way we see the world. They were interested in everything that is hidden, obscure and surprising, like dreams, imagination, and luck. They loved word games and pictures games. In the 1920s, the surrealists were a group of poets, painters, film-makers, photographers and musicians of all different nationalities.*

11

Bird

What are you painting, Mr. Magritte?

In Brussels, Magritte led a simple life. He spent his days painting in the kitchen, next to Georgette's birdcage, took his little dog for walks around the neighborhood, and hopped on the tram for trips into town.

Magritte enjoyed looking like an ordinary man. He often dressed in a suit and bowler hat and he kept his country ways and provincial accent even though he lived in the big city. But Magritte was anything but ordinary. He was a poet.

Look at this painting. What do you see? Is it poetic? Create your own imaginary and surrealist bird, made of something fanciful and surprising.

This mysterious man is a famous villain named Fantômas. Take off your mask, Fantômas! Magritte is a little like Fantômas. Both men are jokers who are also elusive and mysterious!

Look at Fantômas. Where do you think he is? What is he holding in his hand?

Fantômas was the main character of many popular French and American novels and films from 1911 to 1946. He was a masked thief, always followed by the police, but no one ever saw his face. Fantômas was an inspiration to Magritte for many of his paintings.

Knock Knock Knock ...

Is anyone home? There is no answer. Who could have gone through this door? Fantômas perhaps? Like a magician, Magritte paints mysteries.

 Abracadabra! Now it's your turn to make something appear in the hole in the door.

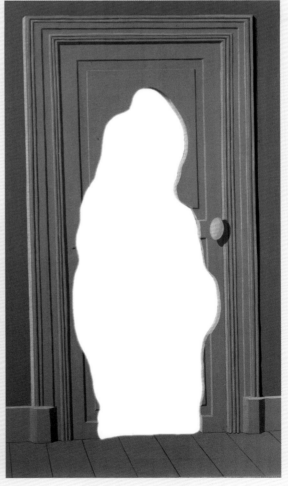

Jingle Bells

Jingle, jingle… Magritte loved little bells. What is hiding inside this mysterious metal ball? Jingle! We hear it but we never see it.

As rain drops

One here, one there… Whenever he can, Magritte slips a jingle bell into his paintings. These are the bells of his childhood, the ones he heard jingling on the draft horses he loved. The little bells travelled and changed…

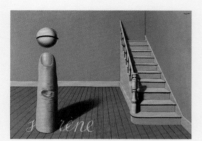

As the dot on the 'I'

 Look at the little bells.

 Now it's your turn to draw a surprising setting for this little bell.

Pipe

'This is not a pipe?' If you think it is, try smoking it! Images and words trick us. In fact, this picture is just a painted surface. With his paintings, Magritte questions everything. He surprises us and makes us think. Why did people start calling a pipe a pipe, and an apple an apple?

Look at the pipe. Does it look real to you, or surreal?

Ceci n'est pas une pipe.

It's your turn to surprise us. Choose an object and draw it in a realistic way, like a photograph. Then continue the sentence by writing the name of the object you drew. Quite intriguing, don't you think?

This is not a ....

'Acacia, Moon, Snow, Ceiling, Storm, Desert…'. Like a teacher at the blackboard, Magritte gets us to repeat after him. In his beautiful school handwriting, he has painted names under each picture. And why shouldn't a glass be called a storm? It is surreal! Calling a shoe a moon and a hammer a desert… and why shouldn't a glass be called a storm?

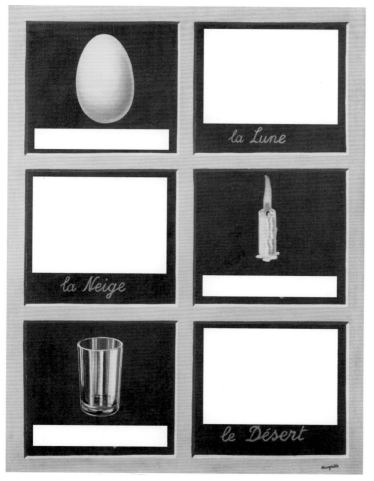

It's your turn to reinvent the names of things. In each empty space, write a word or draw the first thing that comes into your head.

l'Acacia

la Lune

la Neige

le Plafond

l'Orage

le Désert

Magritte

Rainbow

What could be more surreal than painting happy scenes while the world is at war? In 1940, to get away from bombing, René and a few friends moved to a small town in the south of France.

Look at Magritte's Impressionist painting.
Can you see the comma-shaped brushstrokes?

Magritte wanted to paint the sun, the pleasures and the joy of life. In 1943 he started to paint in an Impressionist style. This is called 'sunlit Surrealism'.

Find these colours in the painting.

It's Sunday! The Magrittes have invited their poet friends for a visit. René and Georgette have set up his new paintings in their living room. With the help of their friends, they make up surprising titles for each painting. Someone suggests 'The Ignorant fairy' for one painting. Someone else suggests 'The Key of Dreams' for another.

What a bunch of oddballs! The titles are just another mystery, they often give us no clues about a paintings meaning. The Magrittes loved to laugh and play games with their friends. They dreamt up crazy stories and took photos of each other to go with them. That's Belgian surrealism!

 Magritte invites you to his home and shows you his paintings. With your friends, choose a title for this one.

How Crude!

In 1948, Magritte was preparing an exhibition of his paintings in Paris. He created a new style for the exhibition. He wanted to shock Parisians because they had taken such a long time to like and accept his art. As a joke, he painted works with garish dripping colours. His poet friend, Louis Scutenaire, called this his 'période vache'. That means his 'cow period' or 'crude period' in French. What a funny idea!

Parumpumpumpum! Have you ever seen a rabbit play the drums? Did Magritte paint this gouache slowly or quickly?

Blue or pink period? Rabbit or apple period? Now it's your turn to paint an idea that comes into your head, and to write the name of the period below.

My _____ period.

The mountain is so beautiful! A nest with three eggs balances on a wall. Who laid the eggs? Hidden in the mountain peaks, a *petrified* bird watches with his wings outstretched. Is he an eagle or a pigeon?

When something is transformed into stone, it is **petrified.**

Nothing is impossible to Magritte!
The artist plays with contrasts.
The bird that usually flies through
the air becomes the heaviest thing
on earth: a mountain. Is this
possible?

Just like Magritte, imagine the impossible...

Find these details in the painting. Which ones look like day and which ones like night?

What a strange night! Or is it daytime? The streetlight is lit but the sky is bright. Magritte's painting almost looks like a photograph... or did the artist depict a surreal dream? Magritte painted several versions of this mysterious picture.

Magritte's paintings were very successful. He became a very famous artist. But one day, all the shutters of his house were closed. René Magritte died on 15 August 1967, at the age of 68, in his home in Brussels.

Magritte's last home in Brussels.

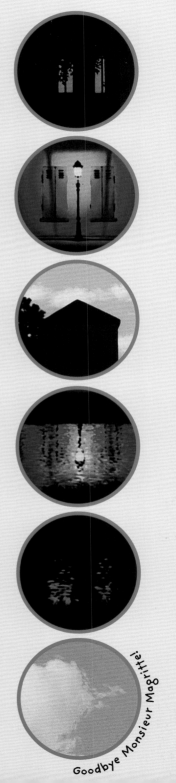

Goodbye Monsieur Magritte!

Texts and illustrations: Catherine de Duve
Graphic design: Kate'Art Editions
Translated by: Wenda O'Reilly, Ph.D.
Proofreading: Nathalie Trouveroy

Photographic Credits:

René Magritte: Brussels: Royal Museums of Fine Arts of Belgium: *The Empire of Lights,* 1954: cover, pp.30-31 — *The Domain of Arnheim,* 1962: cover, p.28 — *The Return,* 1940: cover (detail), pp.12-13 — *The Secret Player,* 1927: p.2 (detail), pp.10-11 — *La Voleuse (The Female Thief),* 1927: p.3 — *The Smile,* 1943: p.3 — *The Great Year,* 1947: p.3 (detail) — *Georgette,* 1937: cover (detail), pp.4-5 — *Black Magic,* 1936-1940: p.5 — *Portrait of Pierre Broodcoorens,* 1921: p.7 — *The One Thousand and One Nights,* 1946: p.7 — *Pom'po pom' po pon po pon pon,* 1948: p.7 (detail), p.26 — *The Rider,* 1922 : p.7 — *Wallpaper projects, Peters-Lacroix Factory, Haren,* 1921-1924: pp.8-9 — *The Unexpected Answer,* 1933: p.15 — *The Forbidden Reading/ Siren,*1936: p.17 — *The Well of Truth,* 1963: p.17 — *Lyricism,* 1947: pp.22-23 — *The Harvest,* 1943: p.23 | **Brussels: Bibliothèque Royale Albert Ier:** *Alfa Romeo - V. Snutsel aîné-Norine,* 1924: p.7 |

Private Collection: *The Son of Man,* 1964: cover (detail), p.1, pp.24-25 — *Toffée Antoine Tonny's,* 1931: p.3 (detail), p.8 — *Midnight,* 1924: p.6 — *The Horrendous Stopper,* 1966 (detail): pp.7, p.11, p.14, p.31 — *Untitled,* 1926: p.7 — *Landscape,* 1920: p.7 — *The Flame Rekindled,* 1943: pp.14-15 — *The Key of Dreams,* 1930: cover (detail), p.2 (detail), p.13 (detail), pp.20-21 — *The Great War,* 1964: p.24 (detail), p.25 — *Clear Ideas,* 1958: p.28 (detail), p.29 | **Los Angeles: Los Angeles County Museum of Art:** *The Treachery of Images,* 1929: cover (detail), p.18 | **Venice: The Solomon R. Guggenheim Collection:** *The Voice of Space,* 1931: cover (detail), p.3 (detail), pp.16-17.

Photographs of Magritte, his family and friends: *René Magritte's parents:* p.2 — *Adeline Magritte and her son René,* 1899: p.2 — *René, Raymond and Paul Magritte,* around 1905: p.2 — *René and Georgette,* 1920: p.4 — *René Magritte standing next to his painting 'The Barbarian':* p.14 — *René Magritte's home at 97, rue des Mimosas in Schaerbeek:* p.31.

© Ch. Herscovici - ADAGP Paris, 2018
De Chirico: New-York: MoMA: *The Song of Love,* 1914: p.10.

We wish to thank Charly Herscovici and the Magritte Foundation, Michel Draguet, General Director of the Royal Museums of Fine Arts of Belgium, Frederik Leen, chief curator of the Royal Museums of Fine Arts of Belgium, Rik Snauwaert, Julie Scaillet, Xavier Canonne, Director of the Photography Museum of Charleroi, Thierry de Duve, Bernard de Launoit, Priscilla d'Oultremont, Chloé Poucet, Joséphine and all the people who contributed to the making of this book.

Did you enjoy this book?
Visit our online website:

www.kateart.com